The Liberty Bell

Introducing Primary Sources

by Tamra B. Orr

CAPSTONE PRESS
a capstone imprint

Little Explorer is published by Capstone Press,
1710 Roe Crest Drive, North Mankato, Minnesota 56003
www.mycapstone.com

Library of Congress Cataloging-in-Publication Data
Orr, Tamra B., author.
The Liberty Bell : introducing primary sources / by Tamra B. Orr.
pages cm. — (Smithsonian little explorer. Introducing primary sources)
Includes bibliographical references and index.
Summary: "Introduces young readers to primary sources related to the Liberty Bell"— Provided
by publisher.
Audience: Grades K-3.
ISBN 978-1-4914-8224-7 (library binding)
ISBN 978-1-4914-8608-5 (paperback)
ISBN 978-1-4914-8614-6 (eBook PDF)
1. Liberty Bell—Juvenile literature. 2. Philadelphia (Pa.)—Buildings, structures, etc.—Juvenile literature.
I. Title.
F158.8.I3O77 2016
974.8'11—dc23   2015032375

Editorial Credits
Michelle Hasselius, editor; Richard Parker, designer; Wanda Winch, media researcher;
Steve Walker, production specialist

Our very special thanks to Jennifer L. Jones, Chair, Armed Forces Division at the National Museum
of American History, Kenneth E. Behring Center, Smithsonian, for her curatorial review. Capstone
would also like to thank Kealy Gordon, Product Development Manager, and the following at
Smithsonian Enterprises: Ellen Nanney, Licensing Manager; Brigid Ferraro, Vice President, Education
and Consumer Products; Carol LeBlanc, Senior Vice President, Education and Consumer Products.

Photo Credits
American Philosophical Society, 8; AP Images: Bill Ingraham, 29; Courtesy of Allen County-Fort Wayne
Historical Society, 21 (bottom); Courtesy of the Bancroft Library, University of California, Berkeley, 21
(top); Courtesy of the Independence National Historical Park/NPS, 20; Courtesy of the Massachusetts
Historical Society, 15; Getty Images: Popperfoto/Rolls Press, 25; Granger, NYC, 16; James R. Mann, 12;
Library of Congress; Performing Arts Encyclopedia, 18, Prints and Photographs Division, 7, 19, 22, 23,
24, 28; The Library of Virginia, Richmond, VA, 14; Missouri History Museum, St. Louis, 4; Newscom:
CMSP Education, 6; Shutterstock: Atomazul, 5, David W. Leindecker, 10, Everett Historical, 9,
f11photo, cover, 27, Rebekah McBride, 17, Ritu Manoj Jethani, 26; National Archives and Records
Administration: ourdocuments.gov/Treaty of Paris 1783, 13 (all)

Table of Contents

Using Primary Sources

Have you ever read an old letter or looked through a photo album? These items help you see through the eyes of people who lived before you.

a boy poses in front of the Liberty Bell at the 1904 World's Fair in St. Louis, Missouri

Letters, photos, paintings, and newspaper articles are examples of primary sources. They are made at the time of an event. The Liberty Bell is also a primary source.

Liberty Bell at a Glance

- originally cast by Whitechapel Bell Foundry in 1752

- recast by John Pass and John Stow in 1753

- currently displayed at Liberty Bell Center in Philadelphia, Pennsylvania

- made out of copper, tin, lead, zinc, gold, and silver

- weighs 1 ton (0.9 metric ton)

- crack in the bell is 0.5 inch (1.3 centimeters) wide and 24.5 inches (62.2 cm) long

Sending a Message

During colonial times it was hard for American colonists to send messages to everyone at once. There were no telephones or TVs.

a 1913 painting of the newly cast Liberty Bell

Instead colonists rang large bells in town squares. Bells were rung to call meetings, share news, and signal danger.

Cast and Recast

Government leaders in Pennsylvania ordered a bell in 1751. They wanted to celebrate the 50th anniversary of the Charter of Privileges. The first bell cracked and broke. John Pass and John Stow were hired to recast the bell. In 1753 they recast it twice to get the sound just right.

the Pennsylvania Charter of Privileges

FACT
Governor William Penn created the Charter of Privileges in 1701. The charter established laws for the colonists.

the State House in Philadelphia in 1752, shown on a map

The bell was placed in the Pennsylvania State House. It was used to ring in important events and gather people together.

Reading the Bell

The Liberty Bell has three sentences engraved on it.

Proclaim liberty throughout all the land unto all inhabitants thereof.

This first sentence is from the Bible. It means people who live in the colony have freedom.

sentences on the Liberty Bell

By order of the Assembly of the Province of Pensylvania for the State House in Philada.

This means the bell was ordered for the Pennsylvania State House in Philadelphia. The words "Pennsylvania" and "Philadelphia" were spelled differently during this time.

Pass and Stow/MDCCLIII

This last line shows the names Pass and Stow. These men melted the first bell down and recast it. MDCCLIII is the Roman numeral for 1753, the year the bell was made.

Hiding the Bell

During the Revolutionary War, American Colonel Benjamin Flower and his soldiers removed all the bells in Philadelphia, Pennsylvania. They wanted to protect them. The British Army was coming. British soldiers would melt American bells into cannonballs.

a mural from 1976 shows soldiers moving the Liberty Bell out of Philadelphia

The American soldiers moved quickly. They put the bells on wagons. The Liberty Bell was hidden under the floor of the Old Zion Reformed Church in Allentown, Pennsylvania. After the British Army left, it was returned to Philadelphia.

the Treaty of Paris, signed on September 3, 1783

The Revolutionary War

During the Revolutionary War (1775–1783), the 13 American colonies were fighting for their independence from Great Britain. Colonists wanted to start their own country and make their own laws. The war ended in 1783, when Great Britain signed the Treaty of Paris. This gave America its freedom at last.

Slavery and the Liberty Bell

Years later, during the Civil War, the Liberty Bell was seen as a symbol of freedom. Those against slavery put images of the Liberty Bell on their signs and posters.

a paper announcing an antislavery meeting in Lawrence, Kansas, on December 8, 1859

ANTI-SLAVERY MASS MEETING!

Agreeably to a call, signed by about 50 persons, and published in the Lawrence Republican, a Mass Meeting of the friends of Freedom will be held at Miller's Hall, at 2 o'clock P. M., on Friday, Dec. 2d, the day on which

CAPT. JOHN BROWN IS TO BE EXECUTED,

To testify against the iniquitous SLAVE POWER that rules this Nation, and take steps to

Organize the Anti-Slavery Sentiment

of the community. Arrangements have been made with prominent speakers to be present and address the meeting.
PER ORDER OF COMMITTEE OF ARRANGEMENTS.
Lawrence, Nov. 26, 1859.

FACT

People who were against slavery during the Civil War were called abolitionists. They felt everyone had the right to be free.

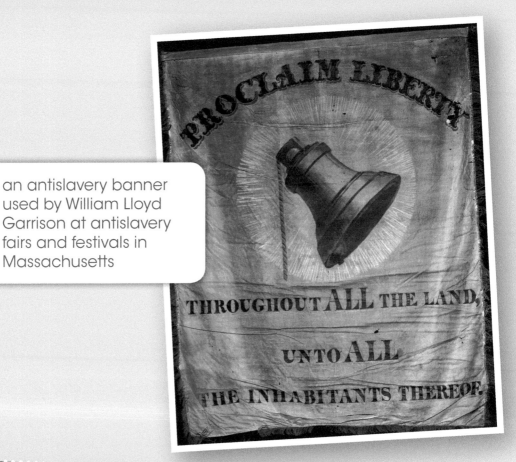

an antislavery banner used by William Lloyd Garrison at antislavery fairs and festivals in Massachusetts

The Civil War

The North and the South battled over many issues during the Civil War. Southern states wanted to make their own laws. Northern states wanted one united country. One of the biggest issues of the war was slavery. The North won the Civil War, and slavery came to an end.

Crack!

The Liberty Bell has a long crack down the middle. Some people believe the bell cracked in 1824, when Revolutionary War General Lafayette visited Philadelphia. Others say the crack was made in 1835, during the funeral of Supreme Court Justice John Marshall. Still other people say the crack was made celebrating George Washington's birthday in 1846.

an 1894 drawing of the Marquis de Lafayette in Philadelphia on September 28, 1824, during his tour of the United States

the crack on the side
of the Liberty Bell

The crack was too big to repair. The Liberty Bell
was taken out of service. Now the bell is only
gently tapped for special events, such as the
end of World War II (1939–1945).

Honoring the Bell

John Philip Sousa was a famous composer. In 1893 he wrote "The Liberty Bell March." Like many of Sousa's songs, "The Liberty Bell March" had no words. Some believe Sousa got the idea for the title because his son was in a parade for the Liberty Bell.

sheet music of "The Liberty Bell March" from 1894

photo of soldiers from Camp Dix forming the Liberty Bell in 1918

In 1918, 25,000 soldiers at Camp Dix in New Jersey stood together. They formed a giant Liberty Bell. They wanted to honor the national symbol.

Students in San Francisco, California, wanted to see the Liberty Bell for themselves. In 1915, 500,000 students signed a petition to get the Liberty Bell to California.

a photo of Blackfeet Chief Little Bear standing in front of the Liberty Bell in San Francisco in 1915

the Liberty Bell on display in San Francisco in 1915

a photo of the Liberty Bell parade in Fort Wayne, Indiana, on July 6, 1915

The bell was loaded onto a train and taken across the country. Everywhere the bell stopped, huge crowds were waiting to see it.

Women's Right to Vote

In 1915 women were fighting for the right to vote. A protester named Katherine Wentworth Ruschenberger had a replica made of the Liberty Bell. The 2,000-pound (907-kilogram) bell was called the Justice Bell. The clapper was chained so the bell could not ring. This represented women's voices at the time, which were silenced without the right to vote. Women used the Justice Bell for their protests across Pennsylvania.

FACT

To help raise money, women sold small versions of the Justice Bell to the public. This helped pay for the protesters' food and lodging.

a photo of the Justice Bell being cast in the early 1900s

In September 1920 the 19th Amendment was passed. This gave women the right to vote. The Justice Bell's clapper was unchained. The bell rang for the first time. The Justice Bell is now at the Washington Memorial Chapel in Valley Forge, Pennsylvania.

Civil Rights

During the 1960s black Americans were fighting for their civil rights. They wanted the same rights as white Americans. They gave speeches, marched in parades, and held protests.

1963 photo of civil rights protesters marching to Washington, D.C.

Sometimes protesters sat in public places for hours. These were called sit-ins. In 1965 protesters held a sit-in next to the Liberty Bell. They wanted to show people that freedom was for everyone.

protesters sit at the base of the Liberty Bell during a sit-in for civil rights

The Liberty Bell Today

Today the Liberty Bell sits across the street from Independence Hall in Philadelphia. About 1 million people visit the bell each year. This American symbol still reminds people what the United States was founded on: freedom.

a photo of the Liberty Bell at the Liberty Bell Center in Philadelphia

FACT

During the Bicentennial celebration in 1976, 3.2 million people visited the Liberty Bell. This is the highest number of visitors recorded so far.

Keeping It Safe

For many years visitors could touch the Liberty Bell. That changed in 2001. Someone hit the Liberty Bell with a hammer and scratched it. Now visitors can only look at the bell from a distance.

Timeline

drawing from 1776 of the Pennsylvania State House

1751   government leaders in Pennsylvania order the Liberty Bell

1753   John Pass and John Stow recast the Liberty Bell twice

1777   the Liberty Bell is hidden in the Old Zion Reformed Church during the Revolutionary War

1824   the Liberty Bell rings when General Lafayette visits Philadelphia; some believe this caused the bell to crack

1835	the Liberty Bell rings during the funeral of John Marshall; this could have caused the bell to crack
1846	Philadelphia's mayor rings the Liberty Bell on George Washington's birthday; this may have caused the bell to crack
1915	the Justice Bell is made
1915	the Liberty Bell is taken to San Francisco
1918	soldiers at Camp Dix make a human Liberty Bell
1965	protesters hold a sit-in for civil rights next to the Liberty Bell

photo taken in 1965 of Liberty Bell sit-in

Glossary

amendment—a change or alteration; an amendment to the Constitution makes a change to it

bicentennial—a 200-year anniversary

cast—to form something by pouring soft material into a mold

civil rights—the individual rights that all members of a society have to freedom and equal treatment under the law

clapper—the metal ball that hangs inside a bell; a clapper hits the inside of the bell to make it ring

colonist—someone who lives in a newly settled area

composer—some who writes a piece of music or a poem

foundry—a factory for melting and shaping metal

petition—a letter signed by many people telling leaders how signers feel about a certain issue or situation

primary source—an original document

protest—to object to something strongly and publicly

sit-in—a peaceful act in which a group of people sit in a place or building to show their beliefs

slavery—the owning of other people; slaves were forced to work without pay

symbol—a design or an object that stands for something else

town square—open public space found in the center of a community

Read More

Eldridge, Alison, and Stephen Eldridge. *The Liberty Bell: An American Symbol.* All About American Symbols. Berkeley Heights, N.J.: Enslow Elementary, 2012.

Gaspar, Joe. *The Liberty Bell.* American Symbols. New York: PowerKids Press, 2014.

Nelson, Maria. *The Liberty Bell.* Symbols of America. New York: Gareth Stevens Publishing, 2015.

Internet Sites

FactHound offers a safe, fun way to find Internet sites related to this book. All of the sites on FactHound have been researched by our staff.

Here's all you do:

Visit *www.facthound.com*

Type in this code: 9781491482247

Super-cool stuff!

Check out projects, games and lots more at
www.capstonekids.com

Critical Thinking Using the Common Core

1. Why did American soldiers move the Liberty Bell out of Philadelphia during the Revolutionary War? (Key Ideas and Details)

2. People believe three events could have cracked the Liberty Bell. Describe one way the Liberty Bell could have cracked. (Key Ideas and Details)

3. Civil rights protesters held a sit-in by the Liberty Bell in 1965. What is a sit-in? (Craft and Structure)

Index